S0-DTA-152

Japanese Design
Through Textile Patterns

FRANCES BLAKEMORE:

Japanese Design

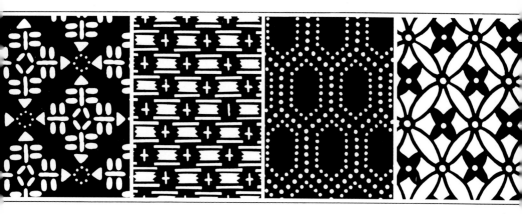

Through Textile Patterns

New York • **Weatherhill** • *Tokyo*

The stencils on the following pages are reproduced by courtesy of the Cooper-Hewitt Museum, the Smithsonian Institution's National Museum of Design, New York City: 61, 66, 78, 95, 99, 104, 106, 110, 177, 223, 230, 234, 235, 238.

First edition, 1978
Sixth printing, 1989

Published by Weatherhill, Inc., of New York and Tokyo, with editorial offices at 8-3 Nibancho, Chiyoda-ku, Tokyo 102, Japan. Protected by copyright under terms of the International Copyright Union; all rights reserved. Printed and first published in Japan.

Library of Congress Cataloging in Publication Data: Blakemore, Frances. / Japanese design through textile patterns. / 1. Design, Decorative—Japan. / 2. Textile design. / 3. Stencil work. / 1. Title. / NK 1484.A1B55 1978 / 745.4 / 78-2430 / ISBN 0-8348-0132-9

Contents

Acknowledgments   6

Introduction   7
  Textile Stencils · The Kimono

1   Water-Related Patterns   17
      Dew · Waves · Irises · Swallows · Fish · Fireflies ·
      Rain · Tortoise · Eddies · Seashells

2   Sky-Related Patterns   45
      Swallows · Geese · Cranes · Clouds · Lightning ·
      Dragonflies · Arrows · Butterflies · Storks

3   Abstract Patterns   79

4   Flower Patterns   127
      Orchid · Pink · Clover · Bellflower · Peony · Thistle ·
      Cherry · Orange · Morning Glory · Lily · Plum

5   Tree and Leaf Patterns   163
      Oleander · Ivy · Pine · Bush Clover · Honeysuckle ·
      Bamboo · Hemp

6   Garden-Related Patterns   205
      Landscapes · Pools · Flora · Fauna · Wells · Fans ·
      Umbrellas · Fish · Turtles · Bats

7   Chrysanthemum Patterns   241

    Glossary   271

ACKNOWLEDGMENTS

Stencils used in the preparation of this book are for the most part those which I have gathered over the years. I am indebted to the following persons for permission to photograph items in their collections: Yoshimatsu Nambu, Tsune Sugimura, Tatsu Watanabe, T. P. Davis, Masukichi Kōgo, and Mr. and Mrs. Michizō Uryū.

I especially appreciate the permission given me by the Curator of Drawings and Prints, Cooper-Hewitt Museum of Design, Smithsonian Institution, N.Y.C., to include in this volume a selection of items from that museum's extensive collection of Japanese textile stencils.

My special thanks go to the staff of John Weatherhill, Inc. In particular I would like to thank Meredith Weatherby for the encouragement and patience with which he has followed the project from its roughest manuscript stages and James T. Conte for carrying the book through to final production.

For encouragement and professional advice, I am grateful to Sara Little Turnbull, who felt that whenever possible the captions should be based on the artist's approach to design.

My special thanks go to T. L. B. for his restraint in advising me on artistic matters while the book was in progress, although on occasion I gratefully do accept his advice and help in other areas.

Introduction

THROUGHOUT CIVILIZATION men have been impelled to leave their marks in the form of designs. At first these were just crude scratchings on stones or inscriptions on cave walls, but over the centuries a vast number of methods have developed as outlets for the expression of man's artistic sensibilities.

The Japanese seem to have had an extra measure of talent in their artistic sensitivity. For them, design has served as a quiet and personal outlet for the humble as well as the elegant. In the development of design in Japan, a profound regard for historical and cultural symbolism was present that led the Japanese to draw visually on their own sources as well as those of the Chinese, and to engage in the continual evolution, adaptation, and improvement of design form.

The Japanese have had, in addition, a special ability to reduce complicated representational ideas to simple forms, and to delight in patterns that are optically tantalizing. Empty space is often relied on as an element of balance, reflecting nature's asymmetry.

For the present work I have chosen the medium of the textile stencil to illustrate Japanese design and design concepts. The uniform silhouette style avoids the visual confusion and pitfalls of color or shading and hopefully will aid the reader in concentrating on the design characteristics of the rich world of Japanese imagination and fantasy.

TEXTILE STENCILS   A neglected and little-known Japanese art form is the *katagami*, the paper stencil used for dyeing cloth. Admiration has long been focused on the gorgeous and colorful kimono, but the basic component essential to the production of such fabrics has unfortunately been overlooked. Yet study of the stencil reveals an artistic influence that extended widely into other arts and displayed something of the traditional attitudes, sensitivities, and poetic capacities of the Japanese. More specifically, a deeply rooted appreciation of nature as it has become abstracted and stylized in Japanese design over the centuries is combined and recombined in these stencils. The Japanese stencil is an elemental form. Viewed alone, it displays a strong silhouette of design components that can be analyzed without the distractions of color values and hues that are seen in the fabrics it produces.

As industrialization has rendered handicrafts the world over impractical, so has the once widely practiced art of stencil cutting almost disappeared in Japan today. Furthermore, the earlier relics of that art are now virtually nonexistent. Except for the few still preserved in museums and private collections, the fragile papers disintegrated or were discarded after use. Today only a handful of craftsmen practice what was once a flourishing art.

The majority of the remaining *katagami* cutters are located around the city of Suzuka in Mie Prefecture, which is considered the birthplace of the art. Through political protection it long retained a monopoly on the craft. Documents indicate that there were a few such artisans there as early as the eleventh century, but this is unsubstantiated. The earliest extant stencils are dated 1689–1703, although designs presumed to have been made by this method are seen in the paintings of the renowned artist Kano Yoshinobu (d. 1640).

By the eighteenth century the technical arts of both cutting and dyeing had been improved, and the stencils were being used on linen and leather as well as silk and cotton. The minute delicate designs known as *komon* and used on silk were first dyed only in monochrome. Because the resist paste used in the process penetrated both sides of the fabric, it was not necessary to repeat the application of paste on the reverse side, as in the case of cotton cloth. Gradually polychrome patterns were introduced by adding new stencils to partially dyed cloth. Later still another system of applying color was invented involving a dye-filled paste which was applied over the resist paste and then steamed to set the color. With this, a number of colors could be applied and set with one steaming. When the paste and the resist were washed off, a multicolored fabric remained.

The stencil survived until industrial methods made handicrafts unprofitable. Compared with the traditional products of this art, today's commercially produced cottons cannot compete with the old vat-dyed indigo-blue cloths which long outlived their owners. Today's few remaining traditional stencil cutters and dyers exist to serve the handful of women who can afford to order custom-made kimono and the few modern graphics artists who apply the method to paper.

It is hoped that this book will afford some appreciation and understanding of the traditional designs that appeared not only in fabrics, but also in ceramics, lacquerware, metalwork, and ukiyo-e prints. As these designs are transformed and repeated in Japanese arts, both current and future, knowledge of their meaning will be of increasing usefulness.

Katagami literally means "pattern paper." The term is an oversimplification of the complicated system of dyeing that related not only to the development of the stencil itself but also to its effective use. The primary factor that made the art possible was a unique type of paper. Made from mulberry fiber (*Broussonetia papyrifera*), this paper has qualities unknown to Western paper of equal weight and sheerness. The first step in making stencil paper was to laminate these mulberry fibers, running them in various directions. The paper was then treated with the astringent juice of the persimmon, giving it the tough brittleness needed to respond to the minute flick of the cutter's knife.

It is said that originally the persimmon juice was allowed to cure for five years, though later techniques were perfected to speed up this process. After the paper was produced, a hard-drying oil was applied to waterproof it and extend its life against the dissolving effect of the water-based resist paste used in the dyeing process.

At the cutting stage a number of pieces of this paper were stacked with the artist's precisely inked drawing on the top. In order to prevent slippage, twists of handmade paper were pulled through holes that had been drilled around the edges. The cutter's blade was then pressed deeply to produce up to eight or nine stencils at one time, depending on the limitations set by the pattern to be cut or the thickness of the paper itself. Some patterns were so minute that they required a thousand openings in an area of a few square inches.

It would seem unavoidable that the brushing of the resist paste across

9

the stencil surface would wipe away the delicate parts of the design, but here again an ingenious solution was devised. A frame larger than the stencil and surrounded by closely driven needles was cross-laced vertically and horizontally with fine silk threads, forming a fine, unknotted netting. The paper twists were then removed on three sides of the stencil frame, and the network of threads was inserted between two of the cut sheets of paper. Using persimmon juice as an adhesive, the papers enclosing the silk were refitted with an accuracy so precise that it was impossible to detect the lamination. The almost invisible threads of silk thus united the fragile cuts in the stencil, and the frame was then cut away. At a later date the last step was avoided by lacquering sheer commercial gauze to the back of the stencil. In both cases the hardly visible threads rolled just enough so that their presence did not register on the fabric when the resist paste was applied.

The finished stencil was then used in the first steps preparatory to the actual dyeing of the cloth. For this, the kimono fabric was laid out on long movable boards. Then a single stencil as wide as the fabric and from six or seven to thirty inches in length was laid on one end of the fabric and a resist paste was applied. The stencil was then lifted and reapplied in succession down the line, the resist paste being painted on each time. The reapplying was done with such precision that interruptions in the design could not be detected in the finished fabric.

The openings in the stencil were the areas receiving the paste and therefore resisted color when the fabric was dyed. As a stencil is viewed in this book, the white areas appear the same on the finished fabric, while the dark areas are the portions that accepted the dye.

The resist paste was made of cooked rice creamed to a consistency that could easily pass through the stencil openings without spreading under the paper. Too much pressure or too thick a paste would destroy the delicate parts. After dyeing, the water-soluble paste was washed out and, in the case of multicolored patterns, new stencils were applied.

A skillful designer worked the pattern in such a way that the components of the left-hand side of the stencil linked with those of the right, greatly reducing the chance of error on the part of the dyer. As the designs were refined, so were new cutting tools devised to perform new functions. Fine steel blades of various thicknesses, curves, and slants—even a hollowed stylus to pick out tiny circles—became the tools of the trade.

For the present book, master stencils involving few colors were selected to illustrate the unity of design. Secondary stencils used for the application of up to six or eight colors are unintegrated and spotty, and thus of lesser interest.

Various liberties have been taken with the photography. Some patterns were blown up to reveal fine detail, while others were greatly reduced to illustrate a complete unit. Thus illustrations disregard the scale of the original stencil except when noted. Occasionally ukiyo-e prints are inserted to show the prevalence of certain stencil themes one or two hundred years ago and to reveal how richly these meaningful designs were combined in the costumes of the day. Because many of these ukiyo-e prints are of actors, designs in their stage costumes were enlarged for visibility and for the contribution that the pattern might make to the role. Versions of stencil themes also appear in still older arts—lacquer, metalwork, and pottery—indicating the common use of these motifs significantly earlier than in the ukiyo-e prints.

THE KIMONO   The kimono was the common garment for the Japanese woman as late as the 1940s. Today Western dress is universal in Japan, though fortunately the kimono is still worn on special occasions. The general drape and cut of the garment have remained the same for decades, with variations occurring only in pattern and color. Style in kimono, in contrast to Western fashion, never revolves around frequent changes in "figure image."

A rigid and complicated set of rules, as well as the unchanging factor of good taste, dictate the proper use of women's kimono. A garment that is fifty years old can be and frequently still is worn today without being outdated. Although new versions in pattern and texture appear seasonally, 11 they do not outmode previous designs. Paradoxically, change hinges not on the age of the garment but rather on the age of the wearer. From girlhood on, in spans of approximately a decade, the number and intensity of colors and the size of the patterns are decreased. Elements in common with the West that enter into kimono selection are the time of day, the season, and the appropriateness of the occasion.

A Westerner may admire a design seen on a Japanese fabric merely for its pleasing overall visual effect without realizing its deep-rooted significance. Over the years single motifs have gone through a series of transformations that often leave them far removed from the original design. For example, the tortoise, a symbol of longevity and traditionally a popular design for kimono, has been reduced to a hexagonal outline. But to the knowing eye, this is still immediately identifiable as the tortoise. The pictorial origins of the Japanese written language may in part explain the ease with which people grasp these visual relationships and continue the use of design classification. Designs sometimes relate to objects that are unknown in the West, such as indigenous toys and tools or articles associated with festivals, the theater, or religion.

A composite of cultural symbols both representational and abstract thus can make up the pattern of an elaborate kimono. The limits are only those of the talent and imagination of the designer. It is no wonder that at one time in Japanese history it was considered quite acceptable for the social conversation of both men and women to center on kimono patterns. Western women in Japan, asked to explain the meaning of a motif in a fabric they are wearing, probably have created many a conversational stalemate either by failing to understand the question or being unable to provide a suitable answer.

Until a few decades ago a Japanese woman's dowry included enough kimono to last for her lifetime, the number varying considerably according to the economic status of the bride's family. But oddly, the array of kimono patterns in the dowry suited only the age of the bride at that time.

It was understood, however, that good Japanese silk could be bleached and redyed each decade according to the graduated requirements of maturity, and every kimono therefore had a lifetime potential. In fact, some silks were deliberately chosen for a texture or a damask underweave that was quite unrelated to the initial richly dyed design. This was done with the future day in mind when the silk might be bleached and redyed a color that would better display the fabric's weave and texture.

Although in foreign countries the label "pure silk" is widely used, such materials often contain a certain amount of metallic filler. This kind of silk is apt to split, rot, or deteriorate after a few years' use. Pure-quality Japanese silks are comparatively ageless. They can and do last almost indefinitely with careful storage and use.

In the West a garment is usually redyed only as a last resort, and even then the result is seldom satisfactory. Seams take dye unevenly, and the overall results are unpredictable if the contents of the fabric are not known precisely. Not so with the kimono. Thirty to thirty-six feet in length and 15 inches wide, the selvaged material is cut into strips and handsewn. Adjustments are made only in widths of the seams. There are no tailoring devices such as tucks, gores, or cutting used for these straight pieces of cloth. The fit, size, and drape that result in the graceful figure of the Japanese woman are achieved through the complicated adjustments of a number of strings and bands tied above and below the waist. Threads hand-sewn along the selvage can be pulled and resewn again in a few hours. Home washing was common practice before inexpensive dry cleaning became available. Every household had a set of drying boards not unlike dining-table leaves; the damp kimono lengths were pressed on these. The raw wood was fine-grained and never filled or painted, thus allowing the fabric to dry with a crepelike appearance which did not require ironing.

While the cut and style of the kimono did not change, there was still much latitude for women to exercise creativity and personal taste as long as the handcut stencil was widely used. It was usual for the customer to examine the wide range of patterns the dyer carried, choosing variations according to her wishes or ordering a new stencil cut to carry out a specific idea. Selection from a fabulous range of colors and fabrics also depended on the individual. Taste was not only exposed in the kimono, but also in the undergarments, which were purposely revealed through the long open slit sleeve of the kimono. The knee-length outer coat, the *haori,* never duplicated the pattern of the kimono but was subtly related to it, as was the haori's lining, which was certain to be observed when the garment was removed.

Sadly, this once fastidious outlet for artistic expression in native dress is now dependent upon the limitations of marketing and mass production. Even the yukata, the soft, loosely woven absorbent cotton summer garment worn by both men and women, is now rarely hand-dyed, although the traditional designs are still favored for the mass-produced varieties. All of this standardization in traditional dress perhaps explains in part the phenomenal growth of "high style" in Western fashions in Japan as the modern woman rechannels her enthusiasm in this direction.

Japanese Design
Through Textile Patterns

ONE

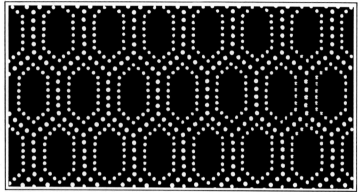

Tortoise-shell design (full size).

Water-Related
Patterns

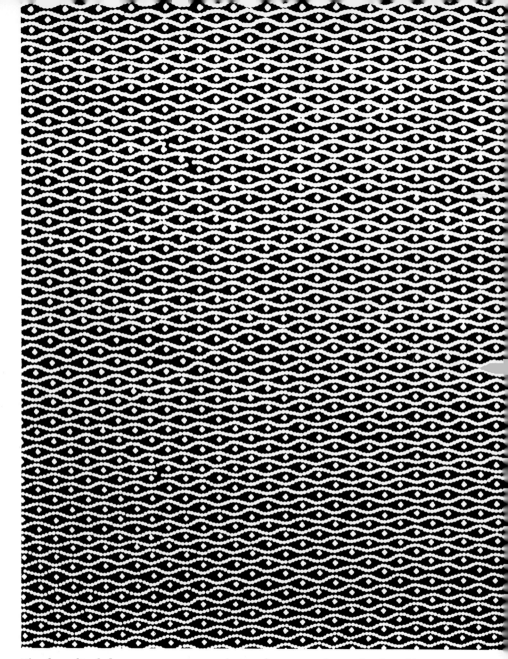

The formalized dew-on-grass pattern shown above was chosen by the ukiyo-e artist Toyokuni as appropriate for the garment of one of his beautiful bathers in the print on the left.

The rhythm of the sea is suggested by foamy waves coupled with decorative drum-heads. In the facing print, both symbols, with the addition of lightning, contribute to the fierceness of the ukiyo-e character.

Irises were said to be effective in warding off evil spirits. From early times this flower was favored as an emblem by the warrior class and the nobility. Transition from the stark white blossom to the black line of waves is eased by the illusion of the grayish tone produced by tiny perforations.

Graceful curves expressing water are common in kimono design. They serve artistically to unite the design and psychologically to suggest coolness.

The silhouetted swallow flies over water between the willow fronds. Note how the changing widths of the horizontal lines are responsible for the background gradations.

Under stylized waves the budding willow fronds are pictured as reflections in dark water. Half of the fronds are inverted to create an identical upside-down pattern, a technique commonly used in kimono fabrics because the long panels that make up the sleeves have no shoulder seams and must appear the same from both front and back.

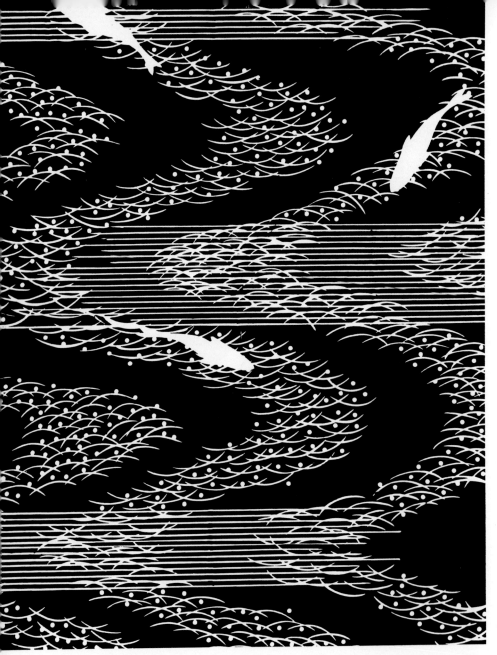

Dew-on-grass symbols not only suggest a shallow marshland but here are also positioned to form a rhythmic flow. The graceful fish are the necessary touch that aids in the interpretation of this otherwise abstract idea.

Mature willow fronds hang over the water. The waves not only flow but also appear to gently rise and fall because of the variations in the widths of the white lines.

The mood of a midsummer night is created by the common Japanese design technique of placing a firefly on the edge of a globe of light. In a pentatych by Toyokuni, fireflies shown in this amusing way punctuate the sky all across the series. In the section shown here an actor holding a cage is engaged in the pleasant pastime of catching fireflies.

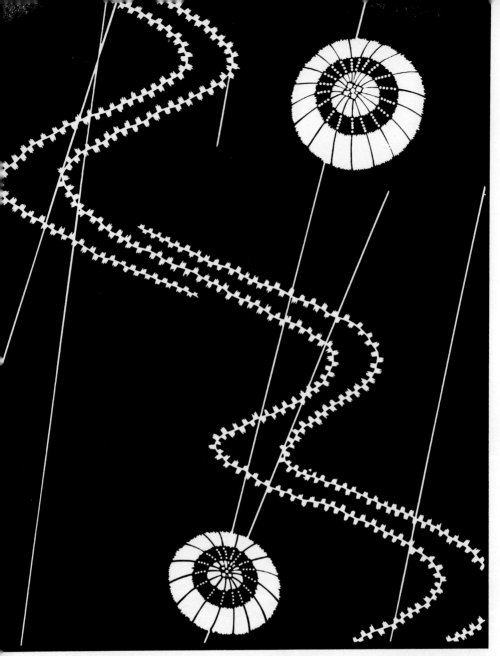

Understatement characterizes much of Japanese art. Here a few straight white lines represent rain striking open, oiled-paper umbrellas (*bangasa*). Wavy water lines flow below.

Feather-edged leaves seem to quiver as they waft toward the water below. Compare how different cutting tools give expression to the wavy lines in this and the preceding plate.

Cherry blossoms fall from the trees before they reach their prime. This notched variety, being scattered by the wind, thus carries a sad, sentimental connotation, like youths lost in battle.

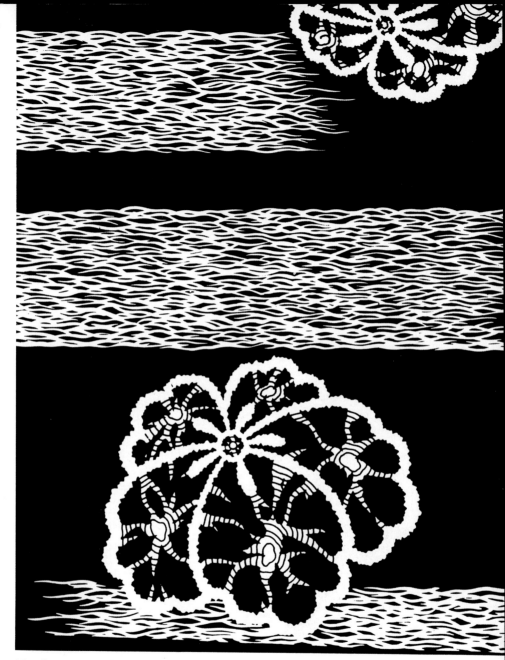

The five-segment divisions of the Japanese ivy (*tsuta*) when viewed full-faced are similar to those of the pansy. The subtly shaded-out horizontal bands are like the much-admired dry-brush technique in calligraphy.

The six-sided tortoise-shell pattern (*kikkō*) may be found in textiles from the eighth-century Shōsō-in repository in Nara through the twelfth-century *Genji Monogatari* (The Tale of Genji) picture scrolls and up to present-day materials. Kuniyoshi makes elaborate use of this form in his woodblock print at right.

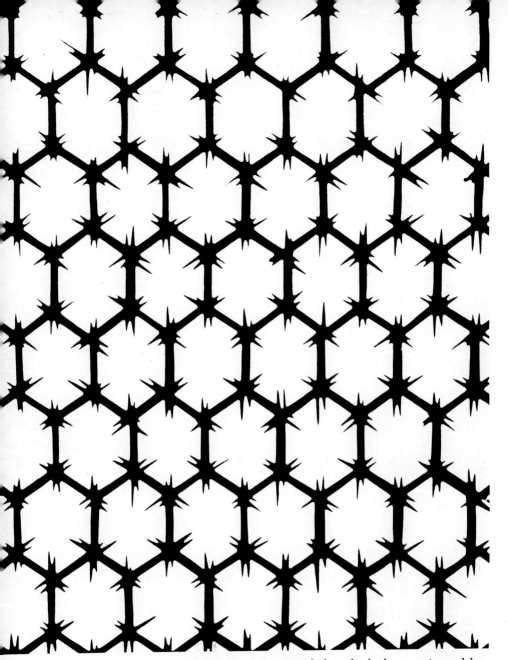

However abstracted, the hexagonal form symbolizes both the tortoise and longevity to the Japanese. "The crane a thousand years, the tortoise ten thousand" (*tsuru wa sennen, kame wa mannen*) is a common proverb.

A good example of bad Western influence on an ancient concept can be seen in this lace-doily effect.

The spiral (*uzumaki*) appears early in Japanese patterns. Kiyomasu used it to decorate the costume worn by the figure at the left. Above is a stencil for a modern cotton print employing the spiral pattern.

Again the spiral is seen coupled with the tie-dye (*shibori*) symbol in the fisherman's costume at the left. Above, these patterns form eddies. The lively imagination of the artist is demonstrated by his viewpoint of looking down on the geese flying over water long before the air age.

The spiral sometimes represents fireworks as well as the swirl of water, but it is never the former when pictured with early spring willows, since Japanese designs strictly adhere to traditional seasonal motifs, according to which fireworks are associated with the height of summer.

The medium of the stencil may have limited the artist but it contributed much to the formalization of design. Compare the spiral design above with those shown on the preceding five pages.

The Oriental method of seeing form in empty space is illustrated here, where the background becomes more important than the mass of seashells expressed in dots.

TWO

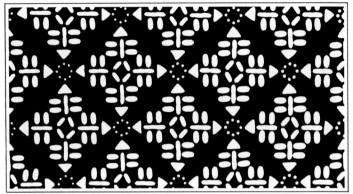

Dragonfly design (full size).

Sky-Related
Patterns

Swallows in the rain, their shadows expressed in hollow dots suggesting the highly regarded art of tie-dyeing (*shibori*). Hiroshige associates tie-dye with the spotted hydrangea on the woman's costume on the facing page—a subtle way of lending overall unity to the textile.

The grace of a bird in flight inspired this traditional, simple brush-stroke style of a goose. The fallen grasses repeat the gentle curves of the bird.

The slender geese stand out in contrast to the medium tones created by numerous flower outlines against dark clouds.

Swallows fly across a bamboo-shadowed stone wall. Here again a change in the size of the cutting tool results in the illusion of vertical shadows.

Not one wing was sacrificed to the cutter's knife in this intricate stencil of a flock of birds—shown here only slightly reduced in size from the original design.

The crane (*tsuru*) has been a part of design and literature in Japan and China since ancient times. The bold stencil above was made for a quilt cover of either silk or cotton. The same crane pattern, but reduced to one inch, is used on formal

kimono as a family crest. Japan Airlines has adopted a simplified version of the crane in a circle as its symbol.

Every Japanese child learns to fold paper cranes, a pastime that goes back at least to the days of the artist Utamaro. In the portion of his print shown on the facing page he chose an exact replica of the birds in the stencil above to decorate the hem of a kimono.

Birds over water are a familiar sight in an island country such as Japan. Kiyonaga uses them on the sleeve of one of his salt-scooping (*shiokumi*) girls in the facing print. Flocks of small birds swoop over water in the delicate stencil above, shown here reduced one-third from the full size.

The propitious combination of the pine, the tortoise, and the crane—all symbols of longevity—can be found in elaborate metalwork on the backs of mirrors

of the Heian period (794–1185). The scalloped shape of the center circle is common to old mirrors.

The boldness of the two-sworded warrior is emphasized by the strong cloud and lightning motifs on his costume. Energy and violence are also expressed in the very old pattern above, where waves are lifted beyond the treetops. Note the faint silk threads that held the stencil together.

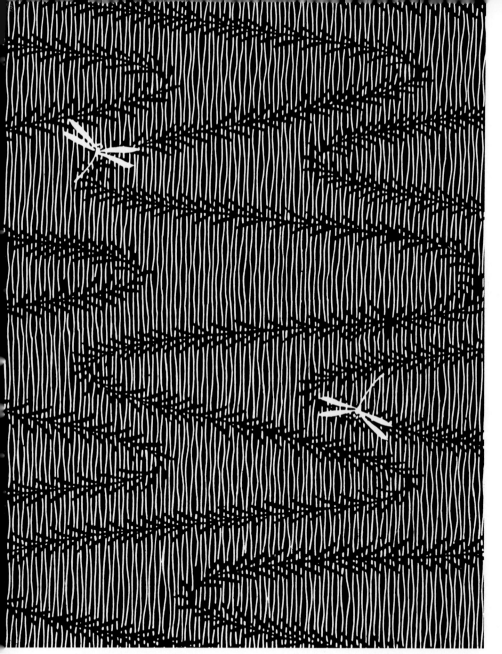

Young willows in the form of waves serve as a watery backdrop for the fragile, darting dragonfly (*tombo*).

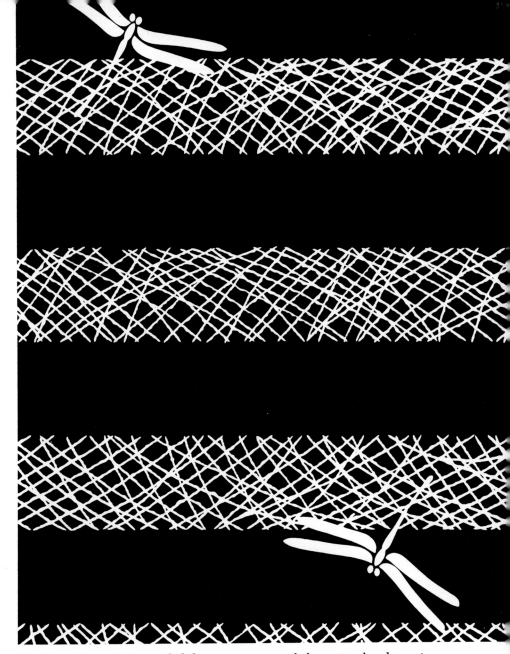

The dragonfly, a fitting symbol for summer wear, helps unite the alternating grass-filled and solid stripes.

Less obviously portrayed than in the previous illustration, the dragonfly seen here is outlined in black on broken white latticework, with an intermediate tone of eddy symbols.

An illusion of shading is accomplished through variations in the widths of lines in both the still water and the sprays of grass that invite the dragonfly.

Children in Japan spend happy hours in pursuit of the dragonfly, using long bamboo poles treated at the end with a sticky substance. The stencil above was no doubt used in making a small boy's summer kimono.

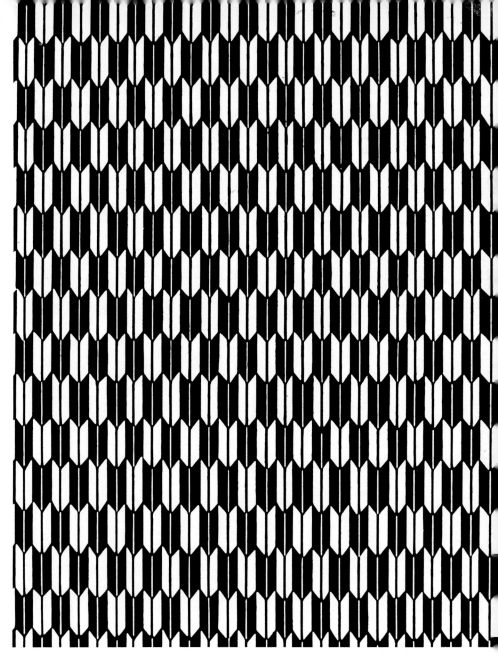

Carried over from feudal times, the arrow pattern (*yagasuri*) lends itself to an attractive allover fabric design by reversing the value of every other image.

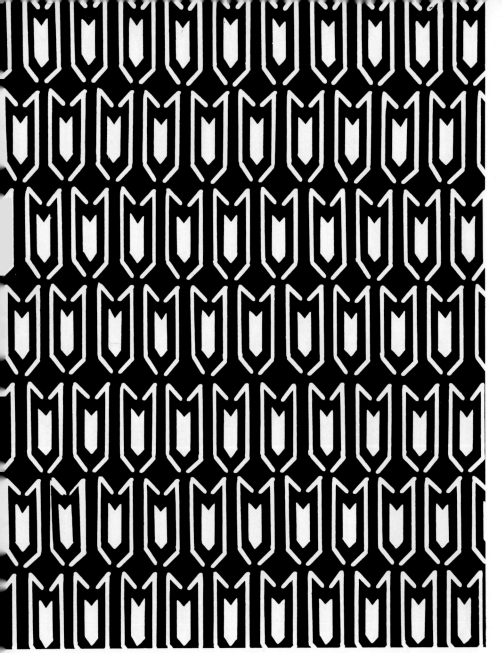

Each row of arrow vanes outlined in white is staggered so that the intervening space in the line below appears to be the arrow shaft.

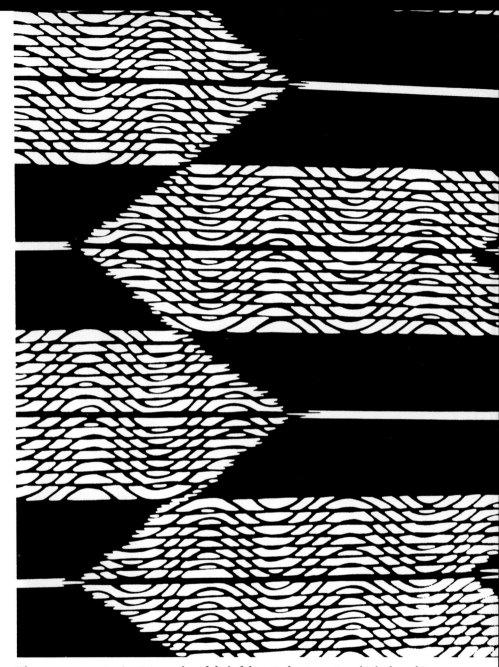

The arrow vane (*yabane*) is another delightful optical pattern in which the white and the black vanes reverse direction.

The delicately serrated edge of the butterfly conveys a fluttering impression in the stencil above. Hiroshige uses the butterfly in the richly designed kimono on the facing page.

The essence of subtle fabric design is the selection of subjects that break up space equally. An appropriate illustration is the combination of spotted butterflies with heads of rice.

The ubiquitous tortoise symbol contains flower and butterfly designs. Note how the artist saw a similarity in the slant of the leaves and the butterfly wings. The above is almost twice the size of the original design.

Again the eye responds equally to the components of the pattern as a result of the free movement in spacing and the skillful design that brings out the similarity between the wings of the butterfly and the leaves of the pink.

The medium of the stencil exaggerates contrasts. The butterflies above appear to quiver against the fusing effect of a bed of dots.

What device is more appropriate to unite nature's patterns than the silhouette of the spider's web, whether looking skyward or earthward?

There is a refinement and simplicity that is Japanese in the understated treatment of the flock of tiny birds above.

The Japanese enjoy representational design so manipulated that the motif is not immediately apparent because of a vibrant effect of light and dark balance. Here sky shapes and storks vie for attention.

THREE

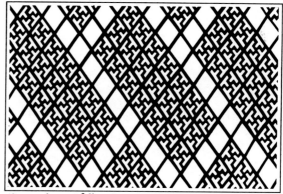

Abstract design (full size).

Abstract
Patterns

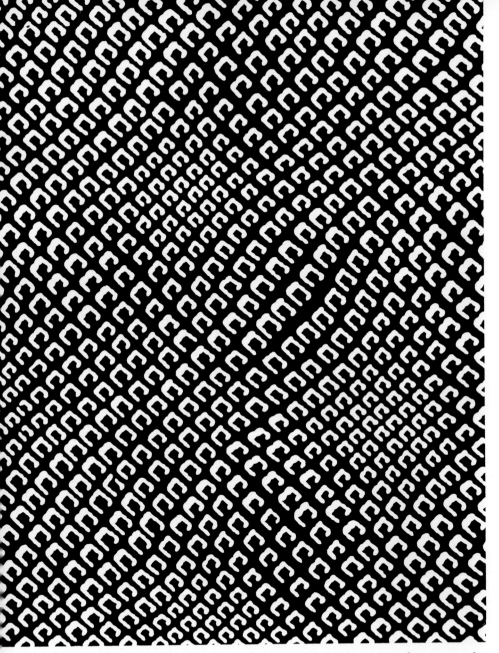

The yukata, a comfortable cotton summer garment, is commonly worn in the evening for strolling or for relaxing at home. Today it is no different in cut from the one illustrated in the facing print. Patterns for men are fascinating abstracts, as in the above stencil. New relationships appear when the eye is focused on either the black or the white units.

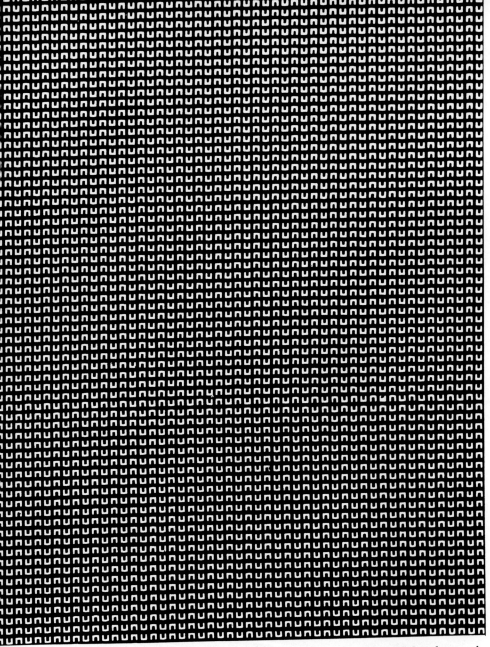

In the print at the right the drooping wisteria is masculinized for the man's garment, while the addition of more obvious floral motifs feminizes the geometric pattern worn by the woman. It is frightening to contemplate the patience that went into producing small patterns such as in the above stencil, where a slip of the knife meant disaster.

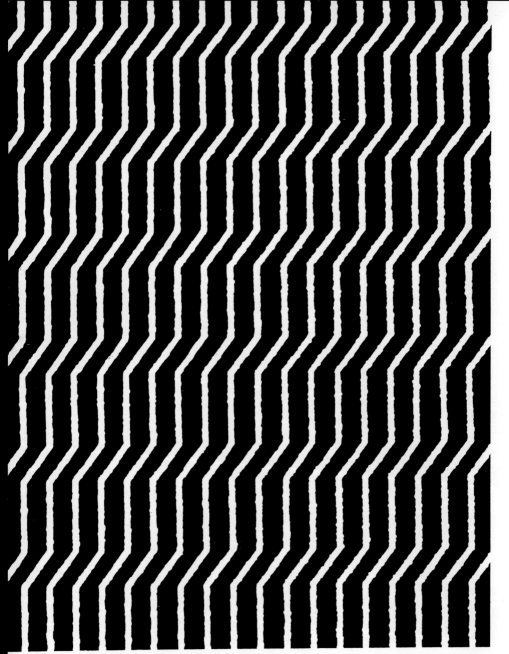

A staggering variety of abstract stencils have been produced for men's yukata. The bold stairlike design above was probably dyed one color, the staple indigo blue (*ai*).

There is no question that the cutter's art influenced design. Without the black horizontal line down the center of the fretwork, the paper would have fallen apart into strips.

Geometric designs were used repeatedly in fabrics as well as on obi. There is a similarity between the pattern above and one of the borders shown in the facing Kabuki print by Toyokuni.

The cutter of this freely expressed water plantain (*omodaka*) stencil had to lift away each irregular white space and ensure that the black images be joined. This reproduction and the one on the following page are twice the size of the original stencils.

Small basketry patterns (*kagome*) overlaid with heavy lines that not only represent the starlike hemp leaf (*asa-no-ha*) but also the stacked pine boxes (*masu*) used for drinking sakè.

A pleasingly textured composition that embodies an array of the stencil cutter's techniques.

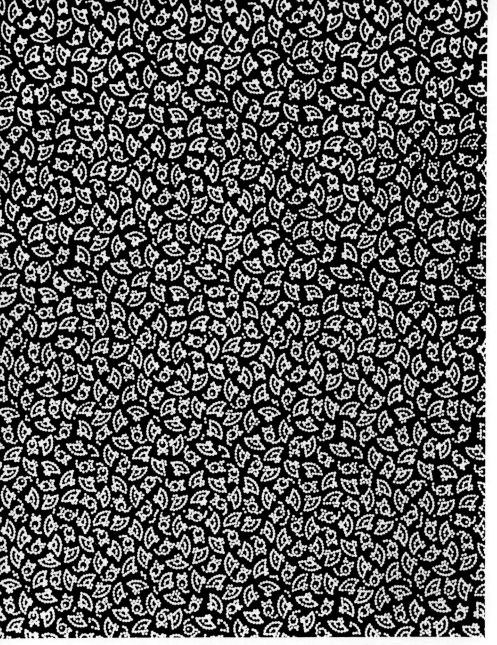

The earliest stencils were fashioned of dots punched out of the stencil paper with a hollow circular stylus. Few patterns are as easy to define as the cat and fan shown in the original size above.

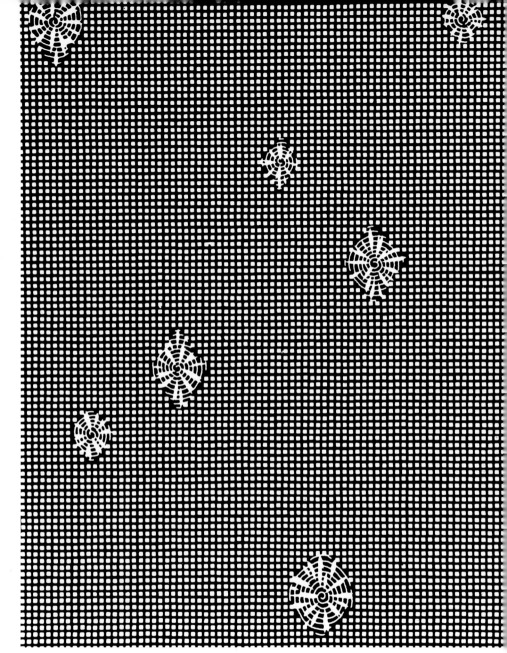

The rigid formality of the checked underpattern is relieved by scattered spirals representing tie-dye.

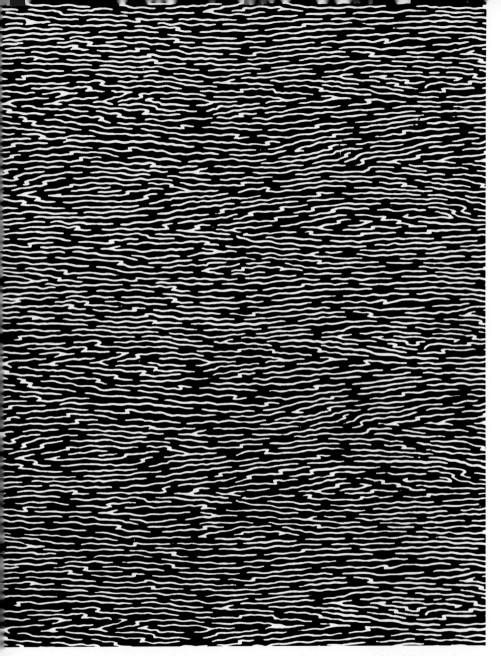

A mesmerizing study in textures capturing the movement of highlights and shadows on rippling water.

At one time weavers wrapped their thread on cards and then partially immersed the cards in dye, giving each thread two or more tones. The dyeing was calculated precisely to result in a desired pattern when woven. This *kasuri* weave, out of reverence for handicrafts, was imitated in the less tedious method of the stencil seen above.

The diamond shape with a flower-center pattern (*hanabishi*) is found with many variations. It has long been a favorite choice for family crests. Kuniyoshi applies it to the overskirt (*hakama*) in the facing Kabuki print. The shoulder and sleeve medallions are mandarin-orange blossoms.

大鷲文吾

This is similar to the Western crazy quilt. All the abstract patterns seen in the random arrangement above are explained elsewhere in this volume.

The above three-dimensional effect produced by line width and spacing is not always an illusion, as when a Japanese roof tile is viewed in a certain light.

The manipulated lattice is basically made up of stripes and squares with slight changes in the motifs that fill the squares.

By controlling the length of the white lines, the cutter has produced the under-
and-over illusion of woven threads.

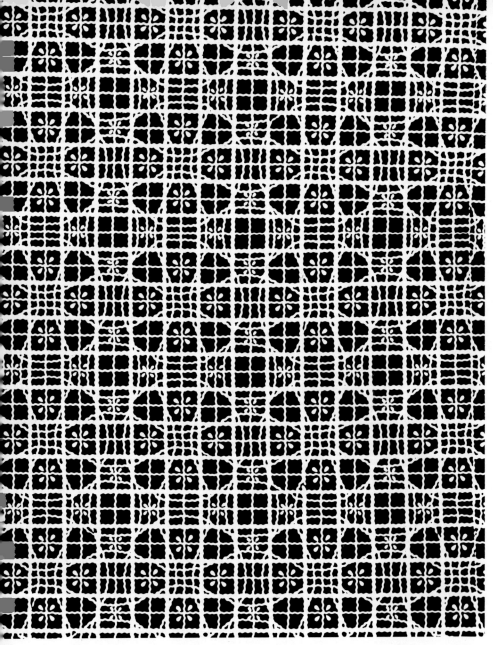

Standard patterns in line cutting intertwine to create new images. Two sausage-like serpentine lines are so spaced as to duplicate their own outline at a lower position in the pattern. A circle is completed by uniting two links of the serpentine. Over this, equally spaced horizontal and vertical lines result in a check pattern. Several interlocking patterns can be found in the woodblock print at the right.

102

The traditional shapes of the counterweights (*fundō*) used on old scales to weigh precious metals form an undulating pattern when laid at right angles. The staggered checks formed by the crossing lines are seen by Japanese as plover footprints (*chidori-goshi*).

The same hourglass shapes as at the left assume a new look as the filler pattern is varied. Despite appearances, the size of each area is essentially the same, demonstrating how line, pattern, dark, and light affect space. This concept can be applied to architecture, interiors, costumes, and every phase of design.

The above pattern is made of perfect interlocking circles. However, the addition of a black spot creates a focal point and transforms the overlapping elements into a four-petaled flower form.

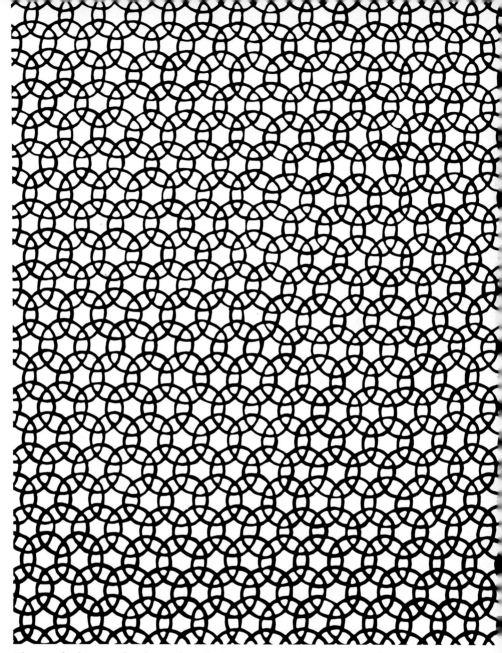

The interlocking circles above, devoid of embellishments, are staggered to create a center hexagonal form rather than the more frequently seen diamond. Formulas that lend themselves to unlimited manipulation have fascinated Japanese artists for centuries.

The Japanese word *shippō* means interlocking circles. It is shown above as circles with birds as well as a center crest. Kiyonaga used the pattern in two ways in the delicate design worn by the lady on the facing page.

It is fascinating to observe how cuts had to be made which still left the paper intact, and the part this restriction played in the end result. Examine how the minute T-shaped cuts in white leave four swastika-like black figures in certain squares.

110

A line version of the key-fret motif (*sayagata*) with the addition of the butterfly, making it suitable for women's wear.

The traditional key fret incorporates the Buddhist swastika, identical with the pattern in the facing woodblock print by Kunisada.

Elements of the key-fret motif can also be seen as a chain in this pleasing pattern for men.

An endless, moving line manipulated to form the Buddhist key fret is here unified by strong over-and-under bands cut out with a larger tool.

The elaborately lacquered wheels found on shrine conveyances are often adapted to overall textile patterns as in the greatly enlarged stencil above. A conventional wheel was used by Toyokuni in a section of the facing print.

Turgid water might have inspired the pleasant abstraction above, producing a cool effect in summer wear.

Three familiar motifs—the flower in the diamond (*hanabishi*), tie-dye, and the interlocking circles (*shippō*)—are rendered in the stencil above.

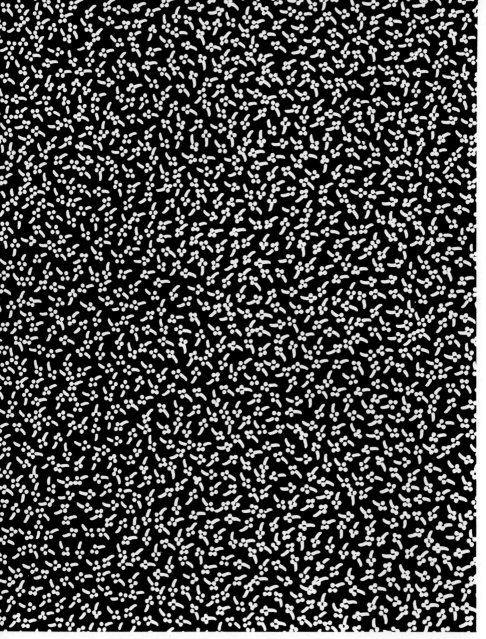

Unwritten but rigidly observed rules still apply to women's kimono. The intensity and the number of colors and the size of the pattern are gradually reduced as the wearer matures in age. The delicate clove (*chōji*) shown in its original size would be an older woman's selection, probably to be dyed in some grayish tone.

These miniature eggplants (*nasu*) shown in the size of the original stencil suggest a dye with a purplish tinge and a wearer a decade younger than the woman who would choose the clove pattern.

The triangular motif above, comprising three hexagons, appears as a linked background for Kuniyoshi's rendition of the mythical phoenix with clouds.

Medallion-shaped cords and tassels enclose symbols of the "Four Gentlemanly Accomplishments," a concept of Chinese origin. The medallion and other Chinese motifs in the facing Toyokuni print testify to the high regard the Japanese hold for China as their cultural mentor.

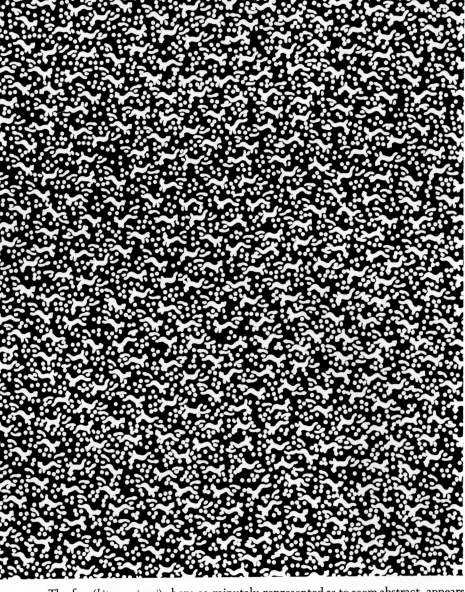

The fox (*kitsune, inari*), here so minutely represented as to seem abstract, appears in fable and drama as having demonlike powers of possession. In contrast, *inari* shrines, which are common even today, are dedicated to a deity known as the fox goddess. It is difficult to guess the manner in which this stencil was used.

FOUR

Blossom design (full size).

Flower
Patterns

Motifs may lose their identity, but the design is often enriched through the limitations set by the tools as well as by the liberties the cutter takes in their use.

The orchid, the plum, the chrysanthemum, and the bamboo were known as the "Four Princes" of Chinese painting, *shikunshi* in Japanese. The prevalence of cultural references in nomenclature indicates the close association between poetry and design.

"The seven spring grasses" and "the seven autumn grasses" are enumerated with a poetic lilt, showing a Japanese facility for recognizing beauty in nature's humblest forms. The wild pink (*nadeshiko*) and the bush clover (*hagi*) seen here are two of the seven grasses of autumn.

The fragile blue bellflower (*kikyō*), effective on a dominant dark ground, is another of the seven autumn grasses. Custom dictates that a seasonal motif be worn at the proper time.

The peony (*botan*) is a native of China revered since ancient times. It is unknown whether it was first introduced to Japan through literature and art or as a botanical specimen. Its complicated form is defined in the above photo, more than twice the size of the original.

Two motifs of Chinese origin, the peony and the scroll-like vine design (*karaku-sa*), said to be based on the honeysuckle, are commonly associated either out of respect for tradition or for reasons of design.

Kunisada captures the elegance of the peony in the detail of his print at the left. This is easily related to the stencil version above, except for the scroll-like treatment of the leaves.

The lowly thistle (*azami*) is appreciated in flower arrangement as well as in textile design, the latter illustrated at the left in a detail of a triptych by Toyokuni. The looseness of the above stencil indicates that it was one of a series intended to allow the over-dyeing of several colors to complete the image.

The notched petal distinguishes the cherry blossom from other five-petaled blossoms. The small flower seen above against a web of stylized branches is known as *himezakura,* or princess cherry. The original stencil is one-half the size of the photo. Kiyonobu I uses the cherry blossom in his "Woman Fingering a Ground Cherry," at the right, made about 1708.

The cherry in metal is used for the sword guards of the warrior at the left, while the double-blossomed variety decorates his costume. The combination of mandarin-orange and peach blossoms in the above stencil is usually associated with the Girls' Day Festival.

Only certain varieties of cherries bloom after the leaves appear. Toyokuni uses one of these in his woodblock print at the right. Above we see both single and double-petaled cherry blossoms. Interestingly, the white ones are shown in a rear view.

Two techniques are utilized to soften this pattern and make it suitable for a textile: the cherry blossoms are filled with unrelated abstract patterns and the sprays are expressed in a series of dots.

A lacy effect results from small flowers peeping through a lattice pattern in silhouette.

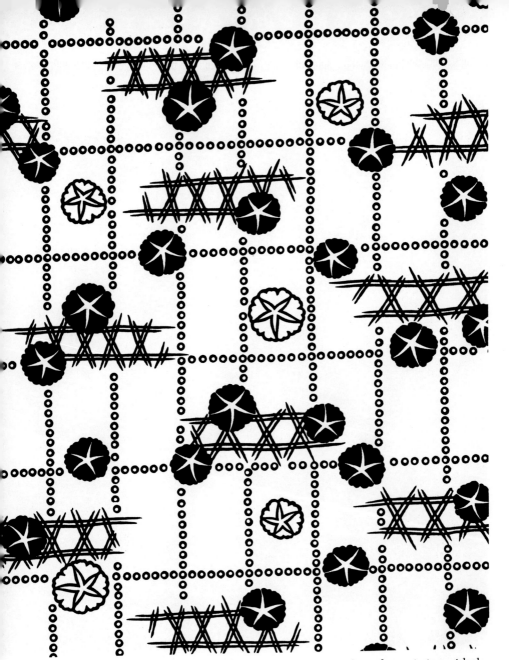

An airy interpretation of the morning glory (*asagao*) in logical association with the trellis. The capriciously placed flowers contribute to the informal mood.

A different interpretation of the same subjects: the morning glory and the trellis, greatly enlarged.

The subtlety in the grouping of the blossoms above can best be appreciated when an attempt is made to locate a repetition. The morning glory used to decorate the kimono of the beauty on the facing page introduces the twisted form of the yet unopened flowers.

A stencil of the lily in silhouette against a ground of daisies.

Here the cutter has followed the style of a *sumi-e* (Oriental ink painting), even to the point of expressing the texture produced by an almost-dry brush as it is pulled away to form a leaf or a stem.

The plum bravely blooms before winter is gone. Displayed both in floral decoration and in design at New Year's together with the bamboo and the pine, it is one of the three plants known as the "companions of the great cold." The plum blossom is the dominant pattern in the kimono worn by the girl in the detail of the Kuniyoshi woodblock print at the right.

152

Toyokuni, in his print on the left, exposes an interesting Japanese facility for looking at things differently: the *ura-ume,* or backside view of plum blossoms, a common design motif. Above, plum blossoms against a faded winter sky. The technique of the latter, while executed in paper, shows a skill similar to that of the early woodcut artists, who had the woodgrain to guide them.

Blossoming fronds of the weeping cherry tree respond to an early spring breeze.

Close scrutiny reveals that a stylus was the only tool used to create the above design. Each circle filled with seven dots is surrounded by six circles with one center dot. Six clusters of three dots surround each circle, making a cogged edge and giving the appearance of a white background.

Above, the jagged-petaled pink in a bed of *karakusa*. A many-petaled member of the pink family is shown here in Kuniyoshi's woodblock print at the right.

These two pages show mated stencils. One was probably used for a faint color and the other for another of a stronger value.

Both patterns are shown in their original size, revealing the skill and the patience that were required to accurately execute detail.

The imaginary flower and the *karakusa* pattern, treated in outline above, were originally Buddhist motifs.

FIVE

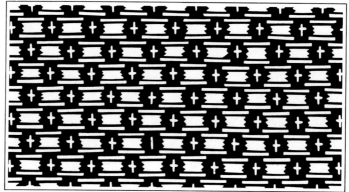

Grove design (full size).

Tree and Leaf
Patterns

Suggestive of Oriental brushwork, the graceful branches of the oleander extend in all directions to form an airy pattern for summer kimono.

Japanese ivy, with its simple five segments, is easily adapted to stylized design, especially in family crests. In the design above, ivy stands out in contrast against a grille of hemp leaf executed in fine crosshatch.

The net motif above serves as a device to rhythmically incorporate numerous abstractions. The Toyokuni print at the left uses the net design as well as the peony and the orchid as part of an actor's costume.

Repeated tree outlines in this strikingly modern-looking pattern are filled with familiar motifs chosen for the tonal variation they lend to one stencil.

The curving trunk of the Japanese pine may appear lost in the stencil above. However, it was probably one of a series of many and was used to accent well-defined color areas.

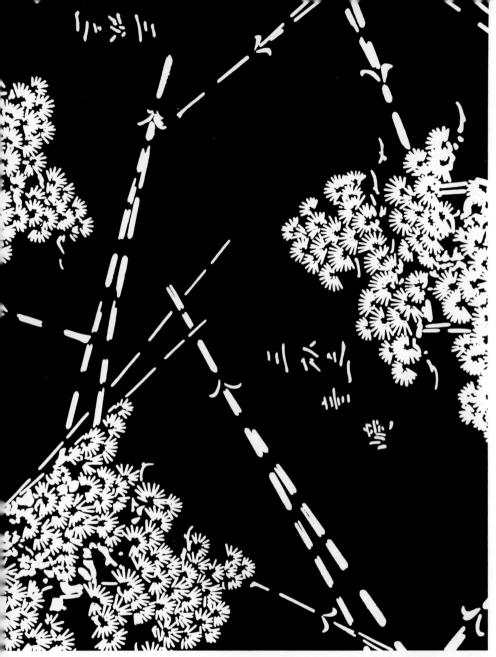

The pine is esteemed as a symbol of longevity, but the needles are valued for a deeply sentimental reason: not only do they grow in twos, but they also remain so until they fall, idealizing the concept of marriage. The disregard for comparative size between the needles and the trees as shown above would not disturb a Japanese, since this is a familiar way of drawing both objects.

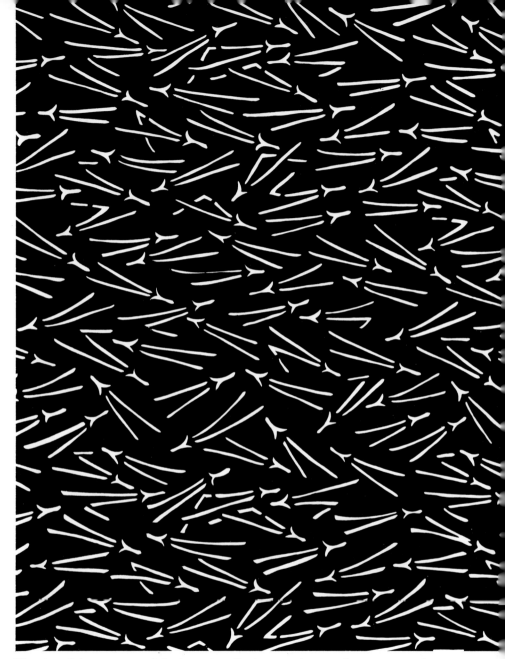

The size of the pattern and the intensity of colors are decreased proportionately as the age of the wearer increases. The happy old lady who ordered the pine-needle stencil above testifies to both longevity and a happy marriage.

The disintegrating silk threads that once supported the paper stencil of the pine above can be faintly seen in the photo of this old stencil.

Two longevity motifs: the pine and the tiny, graceful cranes with different flight patterns, shown in about the same size as the original.

The bush clover above is spaced like a modern painting. Almost two hundred years ago Toyokuni dressed a princess in a kimono using the same pattern in his print at the left.

A more important role is played by the bush clover when shown with the humble water plantain.

While literal and abstract designs do not normally mix, here the bush clover shown against scattered lines seems to be the ideal combination for a soft fabric.

The triple diamond executed in dots above has long been used to represent pine bark. The workman on the facing page has a pine-bark motif on his skirt as well as on his head towel.

The pine-bark motif acts as a window exposing glimpses of nature.

Variations of the *karakusa* pattern may be found in classical and common decorative arts on metal, lacquer, ceramics, or textiles.

The *karakusa* motif used with both real and imaginary center designs. The upper
male figure at the left by Toyokuni wears it in combination with the peony.

The *karakusa* design formalized in a diagonal stripe.

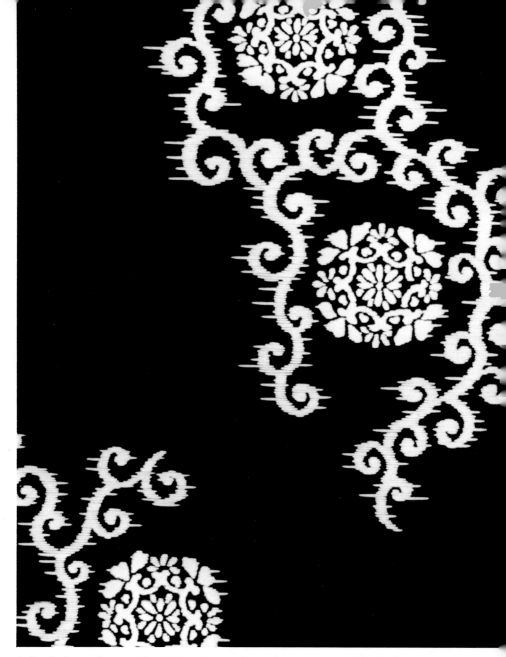

A floral cluster festooned with *karakusa*. What today may seem to be bad television reception represents a technique of weaving pre-dyed thread that is valued for the fused effect it produces.

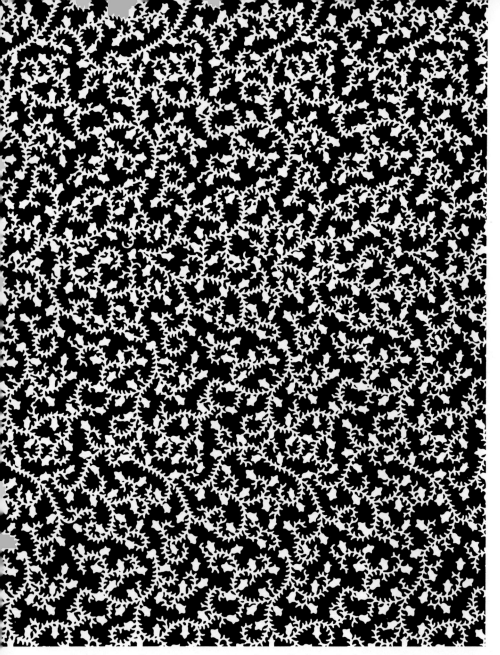

An almost realistic representation of a small plant which assumes the wanderings of the honeysuckle vine.

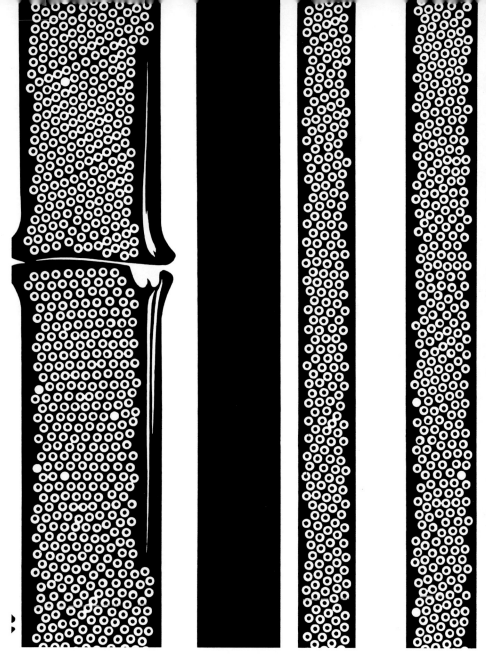

An interesting variety of stripes results from alternating the background white with the foreground bamboo. No two widths are the same.

The decorative curves of tie-dye soften the severity of the vertical shadows of the bamboo above. In Doshu's courtesan the radial leaves of bamboo grass are prominent in the pattern of the kimono.

The extreme dark and light contrasts that appear in a bamboo grove are effective against the small tie-dye spots in the background.

Bamboo grows straight between segments except in art, where this favorite plant is often distorted into a circle for design purposes. Here it is shown against woodgrain.

Small islands may be created by driving bamboo staves into shallow garden streams. The islands become planters and divert water pleasingly as well as provide refuge for small birds. Durable split bamboo was at one time woven into large cylinders and filled with rocks to function as dikes on river banks.

The flexible bamboo plant can be split into threadlike fineness or coarser widths, as in the stylized basket above.

The enlarged bamboo leaves are easily seen in Toyokuni's powerful print at the left. The radial leaves of the same plant appear in a more delicate presentation above.

To make minute perforations in the stencil a small hollow stylus was held vertically and pressed into the paper, a cutter's technique called *kiribori*. Above, the ubiquitous hemp-leaf (*asa-no-ha*) pattern is greatly enlarged, but not nearly as much as in Toyokuni's actor print at the right. For the sake of visibility the designs appearing on theatrical costumes were exaggerated.

Up, down, left, or right, each diamond-shaped segment plays a dual role in the formation of the adjoining six-pointed leaf. Note how the pattern is reversed from black to white in bold horizontal sequence and softened by allover texturing.

Aesthetically suited to textile unity, designs that rely on optical tricks are beloved in Japan. In the hemp-leaf pattern, diagonal and vertical lines carry through while horizontal lines appear only at intervals.

The use of the thumbnail as a tool contributed much to the intricate tie-dye art. A long nail, shaped and squared off at the tip, could skillfully grasp a tuft of silk for tying. The resulting dots of this expensive process are frequently suggested in stencil patterns.

This hemp-leaf webbing is relieved by an occasional leaf cut in white. Less obvious are the scattered ghost leaves accomplished by employing a tool that cut a wider line.

Bamboo segments help form the hemp-leaf pattern above. A glimpse of an undergarment in the Toyokuni print at the left reveals the hemp design richly combined with other traditional motifs that complete the costume.

Dyed material assumes the texture of hand-woven brocade when the formalized design is executed in dots.

SIX

Window-lattice design (full size).

Garden-Related
Patterns

For decades stylized landscapes have enjoyed meaningful and lasting appeal, whether applied to silk, fine linen, or cotton. This stencil probably outlined pastel-colored areas.

Garden pools are provided with small piers and bridges made of staggered planks
in order that nature both above and below the water may be admired.

Tiny punched-out dots imposed no limitations on the variety of subjects expressed in this graceful outdoor scene.

In native silks no other color appears with the frequency of the purples. There are dozens of subtle variations that range from bluish lavender to warm mauves. Are the restrained tones of this color best suited to the long rainy season, the misty skies, and the ivory complexion? Or is it that in Japan nature especially favors these colors, as in the eggplant?

Fans, flowers, birds, and young willows would suggest an outdoor festival to a young Japanese girl. The drums common to this stencil and the kimono at the right assure some happy occasion.

210

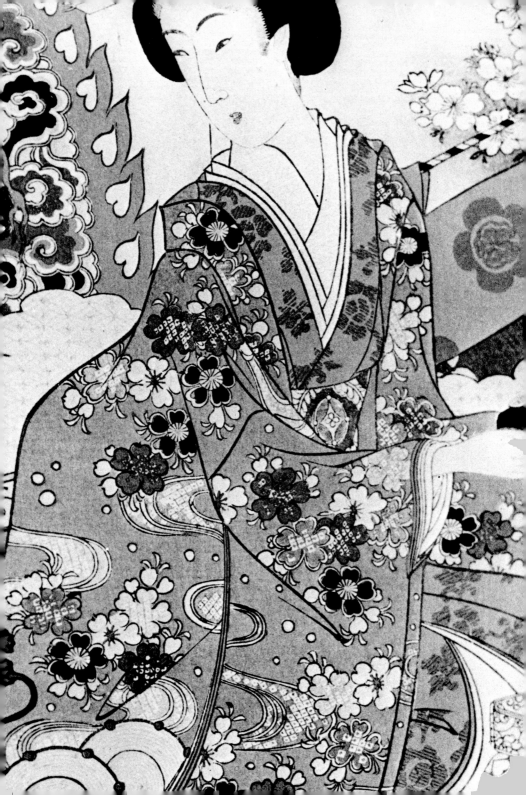

Designated a Living National Treasure of Japan in 1955, the late Yoshimatsu Nambu, through his skill with a thin-pointed knife, earned fame as one of six masters of the paper stencil. At the left we see a section of one of his stencils. Above, an unknown artist silhouettes the same subjects against the sky.

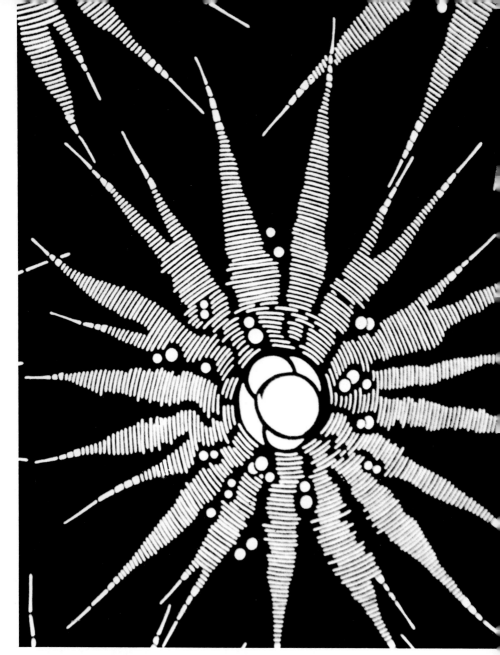

Koryūsai associates the pine, the hemp leaf, and the peacock feather in the wood-block print at the left, more perhaps for the radial characteristics they share than for any symbolic interpretation. Above, a radial pattern representing the tie-dye art.

Butterfly-filled paths, water, flowers, and bridges are represented in this pleasingly abstracted garden setting.

Another garden composition in which extensive use is made of the hollow stylus.

Flowers and plants of all seasons can be identified in the garden print above: maple, plum, orange blossoms, iris, pine, paulownia, bamboo, ivy, chrysanthemum, and camellia, all with a thatch fence. Equally elaborate is the combination of patterns in the costume at the right. Here, with floral symbols and waves, the mythical Chinese dragon appears through a cloud.

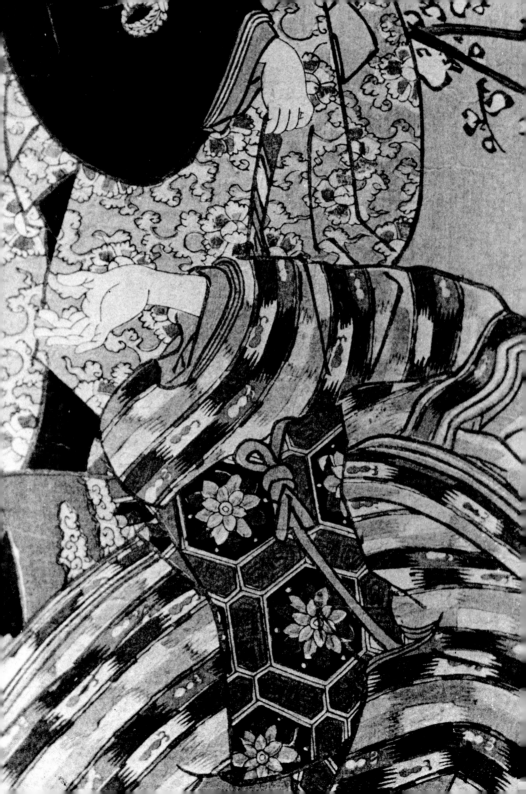

In poetry the ancient Chinese often associated the peony with the Chinese lion, a combination that became *botan ni karashishi* in Japanese. This theme is found stylized classically in the stencil above. Expressed differently, the pair appears in the overskirt of the top figure at the left.

It is difficult to say if a real lion would be fascinated by a peony but the idea has certainly captivated Orientals for centuries. Here the two are associated in a medallion with a *karakusa* pattern.

Crossed double bars resemble the wooden reenforcements at the top of a well and were chosen by the Chinese as the ideographical representation for the word ''well.'' This design lent itself particularly to weaving techniques.

The woodblock print at the left by Kiyonaga illustrates a kimono with the well pattern, possibly hand-woven of pre-dyed threads in the *kasuri* style. Although when the above stencil is used it is much less time-consuming than the weaving technique, the use of the *kasuri* pattern is more an act of reverence than of imitation. The above stencil, four and one-half inches high in the original, repeats the motif.

The flower sprays and fans above, as well as those in the kimono of Kuniyoshi's girl with fan (*sensu*) and iris (*ayame*) at the right, could be worn to a garden-viewing party.

The Japanese have a deep affection for the durable and attractive bamboo crafts. It is thus natural that these be represented in textile design as in the fan-rib grid above and the oiled-paper umbrella in Kunisada's figure on the facing page.

The large oiled-paper umbrella was at one time seen everywhere in Japan, especially during the rainy season. Here it is associated with water symbols and pine clusters.

The snowy heron (*sagi*) in a cool watery spot is a fitting design for a summer kimono. The delicate script running at right angles works in subtly as part of the landscape.

Lettering on fabric cannot be attributed to recent Western fads, for it has long been used in the Orient. From slogans and trademarks on workers' garments to poetry on elegant fabrics, it easily blends into the design. The handsome samurai at the right by Toyokuni III wears a script-filled garment.

232

The odor of charcoal-broiled seafood is common to garden restaurants in Japan. This very modern-looking lobster was in fact designed years go.

The maple leaf mirrored in a rippling stream gives the opportunity to introduce color into a strong rhythmic presentation.

While the spiral wave design is universally similar to that above, the abstracted wave in Japan resembles the scales of the fish as depicted here. Variations of the scale design (*uroko moyō*) were used in fabrics as talismans against evil.

Rare and expensive variegated carp are the attraction in the ponds of many temples and well-kept gardens. Here they swirl under the reflection of overhanging foliage.

Turtles in a garden pond could have inspired this merry grouping.

The turtle with a tail of water plants is not uncommon in Japanese art. It is said that certain freshwater turtles carry such growth as camouflage.

Japanese reverence for all living things embraces creatures seldom glorified in the West, even insects and rodents. These ornamental bats would have been appropriate on a midnight-hued silk.

240

SEVEN

Chrysanthemum design (full size)

Chrysanthemum
Patterns

The Japanese imperial crest, the formalized chrysanthemum with sixteen petals, is said to have evolved from a sun emblem associated with the mythological ancestor of the Japanese, the sun goddess. In veneration of the sun, which symbolizes the highest of all things, it was supposedly adopted as the emblem of the imperial line in the twelfth century. Today the chrysanthemum is considered the national flower of Japan.

The actual plant, as well as the fables and literature associated with it, was first introduced into Japan from China in the eighth century. The Japanese have since developed this amazing flower until there are now said to be over five thousand varieties grown in as many sizes, shapes, and colors—some of which may be found blooming in any season.

Chrysanthemums are used repeatedly in the art of flower arrangement, an accomplishment to which every Japanese woman has at least had some exposure. Through the years, chrysanthemums have been competitively grown and elaborately displayed indoors and outdoors until today viewing such flower exhibits is a national pastime. Large floral sculptures, made of hundreds of blossoms grown to resemble both popular and historical subjects and figures, are one such attraction. Frequently blossoms are so enormous as to require bamboo or wire braces for support. In late autumn potted chrysanthemum cascades of hundreds of tiny flowers are offered for sale everywhere. Designed for the container to be placed in an elevated position so that the shower of blossoms may reach out and tumble down for several feet, this popular arrangement is highly valued.

The Japanese shared the ancient Chinese belief that longevity was assured for those who drank a brew made from the plant or who drank from a stream in which the dew from the chrysanthemum had fallen. Literature and poetry abound with auspicious references to this flower, and even today some older people, although having faith in more modern scientific methods, can cite some of the home remedies their forebears made from the plant and recount the cures these were supposed to effect. The flower is even used as a food, and anyone who has tried a yellow chrysanthemum blossom fried in deep fat with tempura or tasted a few tangy petals with cold slices of raw fish will agree to the flower's suitability as a condiment.

Needless to say, this noble flower has served as an inspiration for many textile patterns—from the heavily embroidered imperial-court costumes of the past to the simplest cottons of modern times. The present chapter is illustrated with stencils in which this flower plays a dominant role. While tradition dictates that the wearing of nature's symbols conform strictly to the season of the year, the chrysanthemum is considered a flower for all seasons.

The stencil cutter removes the white areas in a pattern. When the background is predominantly dark (*jizomari*), as in the stencil above, his work is much easier but no less effective.

Despite their stylized diamond form, the above flowers would be immediately recognized by a Japanese as being chrysanthemums.

Several species of chrysanthemums in a Yoshimatsu Nambu (see page 213) master-piece.

Treated in outline, graceful groupings of chrysanthemum sprays lean diagonally both up and down over water. Chrysanthemum outlines are seen in the garment of the musician at the left.

The dark blossoms of these chrysanthemums were probably dyed in ranges of russet and purple. Compare the variety of treatments given the centers of the blossoms.

Twisting petals of the scraggly species of this beloved national flower of Japan.

The above cutting technique, where the background is predominantly white, is
called *jishiro*.

Whatever the season, some variety of chrysanthemum can be found. Here some appear with *yaezakura,* a double-blossomed cherry that blooms in the spring after the tree's leaves come out.

The delicate line of the spray of small flowers provides a third tone in contrast to the bolder white chrysanthemums.

An elegant presentation built around formalized chrysanthemums.

According to Chinese legend, one hundred years of life were assured those who drank from a stream lavishly banked with chrysanthemums. The fourteenth-century scholar-warrior Kusunoki Masashige adopted chrysanthemum and water symbols as his crest. The artist Kuniyoshi did the facing portrait of Kusunoki, showing this crest on both his kimono and the lacquered stool. Various versions of this combination of symbols can be found in kimono design.

257

Swallows flying through formalized snowflakes become a visual haiku. Coupled with sprigs of the chrysanthemum, the flower for all seasons, an element of fantasy is added.

The artist takes full advantage of this luxuriously petaled species, which droops
in irregular shapes. The Japanese are said to have developed over five thousand
varieties of this many-petaled flower in a myriad of colors and forms.

The designer shares nature's talent in making the above arrangement seem un-
studied. There is a similarity of treatment in the careless grouping of the flowers
above and those in Kuniyoshi's sensitive print at the right.

The mass effect above suggests the variety of chrysanthemum trained in pots to cascade down from a pedestal. White, yellow, and russet arrangements are commonly displayed in autumn.

The deliberate, studied naturalness that can be observed in formal Japanese flower arrangement carries over to the spacing of the chrysanthemums above.

On a formal black woman's kimono a mass of colorful designs similar to the group above might appear in the skirt. In the days of the gentleman at the left, the chrysanthemum was lavishly used from the breast down, with the contrasting family crest placed on the dark areas of the shoulders and sleeves.

The uniqueness of the above pattern lies in the choice of a species with swirling petals.

The pattern at the left is close to the size of the original. The enlargement of
the same stencil shown above demonstrates how size affects impact.

The single-petaled chrysanthemum mixes easily with the more ornate design of the peony. The ubiquitous *karakusa* pattern loosely fills the background.

To serve the requirements of a medium-toned textile, a head-on view of a mass of chrysanthemums is employed.

To flick away tiny bits of paper and yet preserve the continuity of each petal exemplifies the difference between the arts of the cutter and the designer. A skilled painter could brush in the petals of this spiderlike species in minutes, but it is impossible to estimate the time it took for the cutter to produce this stencil.

Glossary-Index

ai (indigo blue), 84

asagao (morning glory), 146

asa-no-ha (hemp leaf), 89, 196

ayame (iris), 226

azami (thistle), 137

bangasa (oiled-paper umbrella), 30

botan (peony), 132, 221

chidori-goshi (plover-footprint pattern), 104

chōji (clove), 120

Doshu (fl. c. 1715), ukiyo-e painter, 189

fundō (counterweights), 104

hagi (bush clover), 130

hakama (divided skirt), 96

hanabishi (flower-in-a-diamond pattern), 96, 119

haori (knee-length outer coat), 14

himezakura (princess cherry), 138

Hiroshige (1797–1858), ukiyo-e painter, printmaker, 47, 70

inari (fox), 126

jishiro (stencil-cutting technique in which most of the background is cut away), 252

jizomari (stencil-cutting technique in which most of the background is left intact), 244

kagome (woven-basket pattern), 89

karakusa (any of a variety of scroll-like vines), 133, 158, 162, 181, 183, 184, 185, 222, 268

kasuri (dyeing and weaving technique in which thread was wrapped around cards, which were then partially immersed in dye, giving each thread two or more tones; the dyeing was calculated precisely to result in a desired pattern when woven), 95, 225

katagami (paper stencils used for dyeing cloth), 7–11

kikkō (tortoise shell), 34

kikyō (bellflower), 131

kiribori (using small hollow stylus to punch out holes in stencil), 196

kitsune (fox), 126

Kiyomasu (fl. 1696–1716), ukiyo-e printmaker, 39

Kiyonaga (1752–1815), ukiyo-e painter, printmaker, 57, 109, 225
Kiyonobu I (1664–1729), ukiyo-e painter, printmaker, 138
Koryūsai (fl. c. 1764–88), ukiyo-e painter, printmaker, 215
Kunisada (also known as Toyokuni III; 1786–1864), ukiyo-e painter, printmaker, 113, 135, 228
Kuniyoshi (1797–1861), ukiyo-e painter, printmaker, 34, 96, 122, 152, 158, 226, 257, 260
masu (pine box used for drinking sakè), 89
nadeshiko (wild pink), 130
Nambu, Yoshimatsu (1894–1976), master stencil cutter, 213, 247
nasu (eggplant), 121
omodaka (water plantain), 88
sagi (snowy heron), 231
sayagata (key-fret design), 111
sensu (folding fan), 226
shibori (tie-dye), 41, 47
shikunshi (the Four Princely Plants—plum, bamboo, chrysanthemum, and orchid), 129
shiokumi (person scooping salt water), 57
shippō (interlocking circles), 109, 119
sumi-e (Oriental ink painting), 151
tombo (dragonfly), 62
Toyokuni (1769–1825), ukiyo-e painter, printmaker, 19, 28, 86, 116, 124, 137, 142, 155, 167, 175, 183, 195, 196, 203
Toyokuni III (see Kunisada), 232
tsuru (crane), 52
tsuta (ivy), 33
ura-ume (backside view of a plum blossom), 155
Utamaro (1754–1806), ukiyo-e painter, printmaker, 54
uroko moyō (fish-scale design), 236
uzumaki (spiral, eddy, whirlpool), 39
yabane (arrow vane), 69
yaezakura (double-blossomed cherry), 253
yagasuri (arrow-feather design), 67